CHARLES ALBERT BENDER

National Hall of Fame Pitcher

KADE FERRIS

MINNESOTA NATIVE AMERICAN LIVES SERIES

ISBN 13: 978-1-63489-365-7
Library of Congress Catalog Number: 2020913770
Printed in the United States of America
First Printing: 2020

24 23 22 21 20   5 4 3 2 1

Illustrations © 2020 Tashia Hart
Book design by Patrick Maloney
Back cover photo: Bain News Service, Publisher. *Chief Bender, Philadelphia AL baseball.* 1913. Photograph. www.loc.gov/item/2014697519.

This work is funded with money from the Arts and Cultural Heritage Fund that was created with the vote of the people of Minnesota on November 4, 2008.

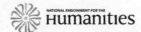

Wise Ink Creative Publishing
807 Broadway St. NE, Suite 46
Minneapolis, MN 55413
wiseink.com

To order, visit itascabooks.com or call 1-800-901-3480. Reseller discounts available.

CONTENTS

INTRODUCTION

Storytelling is a traditional tool of many Indigenous people, and here in Minnesota our storytelling tradition is alive and well among Native Americans of many nations. The authors, illustrators, and editors of this series, who are all Dakota or Ojibwe, continue their cultural traditions in creating these books.

The Minnesota Humanities Center and the editors of this series of books for younger readers believe it is important to envision the future through stories of the past and present. Our goal is to help Native American children see their cultures represented alongside biographies of other leaders in our larger society. We envisioned a series of children's books by, for, and about Dakota and Anishinaabe (Ojibwe) and other Indigenous people, portraying our histories, knowledge ways, culture keepers, and beloved figures. These biographies are meant to help Dakota, Anishinaabe, and other Native American children imagine their own potential for full futures.

Of all the children's books published in the United States, only 1 percent are written by Native and First Nations authors, according to the Cooperative Children's Book Center at the University of Wisconsin–Madison.[1]

---

1 Data on books by and about people from First/Native Nations published for children and teens compiled by the Cooperative Children's Book Center, School of Education, University of Wisconsin–Madison. ccbc.education.wisc.edu/books/pcstats.asp

Our hope is that teachers and parents will encourage young readers to see themselves in the extraordinary lives presented in these stories. We also hope readers will consider how the facts of social barriers based in race, culture, education, and class influenced the lives of the subjects of these books. History, especially the impacts of treaties, underlies these stories as well. These are narratives that open up contexts of language and culture and the policies meant to destroy them. The legacy of boarding schools and forced education away from family figures into each story to some extent. Poverty and the disruption of family life are also themes too many children can relate to, and the women and men featured in these narratives overcame just such circumstances.

The first books in this series include stories of historic figures who lived, worked, and broke barriers a hundred years ago, as well as the ongoing story of an exceptional Ojibwe woman who rose to the highest levels of leadership in Minnesota and in the nation.

—Gwen Nell Westerman and Heid E. Erdrich,
series editors, May 2020

Chapter One

FROM THE FORESTS TO THE FIELDS

How many times have you given something your best effort? We all want to win, but is winning all there is? Sometimes, just knowing you've given your best effort, even if you lose, is enough. Hard work and dedication matter more than simply winning. This idea defined the life of Charles Albert Bender.

Charles was born in 1884 along a small lake near Brainerd, Minnesota. His father, Albertus, was a German American who came to Minnesota to be a lumberjack. His mother, Mary Razor, was an Ojibwe woman from the Mississippi Band. He was the fourth of eleven children.

Life there was tough and Mr. and Mrs. Bender both had to work long hours. Along with the other lumberjacks, Mr. Bender cut wood all day long and Mrs. Bender worked as a cook for the men. Even though life was a challenge, they were able to make a living for a few years until all the trees were cut. Once the trees were gone, the family packed up and moved west to the White Earth Reservation, looking for new opportunities.

At White Earth, the Bender family hoped to start a farm. They were able to get land to homestead, but most of the good land had already been taken by other tribal members and white settlers. This meant they had to settle for a poor patch of land that was swampy, hilly, and full of rocks.

The Benders had a hard time starting out and struggled to make ends meet. "We had a hard time of it," Charles once said of his childhood growing up on the farm. Farming was a family job. Everyone had to do their part. Charles's job was to hand-pick rocks from the ground in front of the plow to make planting easier. He would walk along the plow's path and pick up stones. He would then throw them out of the field to where they wouldn't hurt the plow or the horses that pulled it. It was hard work, but after a while, Charles had built a very good arm. He could hit almost everything he wanted when throwing rocks. "That is how I laid my foundation as a pitcher," he once recalled when thinking back to his childhood.

Even though everyone helped out the best they could, the Benders struggled to feed all members of the family. So, when he was seven years old, it was decided that Charles and his siblings needed to be in school, where they could get at least one meal a day. At that time, the schools on the White Earth Reservation were very crowded and Mr. and Mrs. Bender could not get a spot for their children. Because of this, they decided to send their children to a boarding school in Pennsylvania, where they could stay and learn. Charles, his brother John, and his sister Anna were given tickets and put on a train headed east. They rode for several days before they finally arrived at the Lincoln Institution near Philadelphia, Pennsylvania.

Chapter Two

GRADE SCHOOL DAYS

The Lincoln Institution, like most Indian boarding schools, was created by the US government to make Native American children adapt to white society. The hope was that by taking Native children out of their communities and teaching them to be like white men, they would leave their traditional ways behind. Some people believed Native Americans could be "civilized" only by taking children from the reservation and putting them far away from their friends and families. Then, once they were away, they could learn the English language, work trade jobs for a living, and become just like the white man.

Charles soon found that life at the school was a lot like being in the military. He and the other students had to wake up early in the morning, make their beds, and dress in uniforms. Before they got their breakfast, they were made to march in formation and do exercises. Then students lined up to say the Pledge of Allegiance to the American flag. After breakfast, students were taught subjects such as English and math, and did chores at the school's farm. They also milked cows and planted and harvested crops.

Like most students, Charles and his brother and sister were not allowed to go home. If they were lucky, they were allowed a few visits from family members. But, because Charles's family was poor, they went many years without seeing them. Finally, when he was twelve,

Charles was sent home to his family at White Earth. He had spent five years at the Lincoln Institution.

When he arrived home, Charles was supposed to be old enough to work on the farm. He was happy to see his family, but the work was hard. There were also now thirteen people living in their small home. He was miserable.

One day, he and his brother John were asked to get water for the house. It was quite a way to walk to get the water. He was slow in getting it, and his father got angry at them. In his anger, his father kicked Charles and he fell, spilling the water. His father demanded Charles and John go back to get more. This was unfair, and Charles became angry. He and his brother decided to run away from home. They ran several miles until they came to a relative's farm. When they got there, they refused to go home.

Not too long after that, a teacher from the Carlisle Indian Industrial School came to White Earth. He was there to recruit students to come to this new boarding school. While visiting homes, the man met Charles and John. He told them they could attend if they wanted to. This made Charles very happy. He had enjoyed school when he was at the Lincoln Institution. He liked learning and he thought it was better than having to live in his crowded home. So, Charles accepted the offer and was soon back on a train to Pennsylvania on September 5, 1896.

Chapter Three

CARLISLE SCHOOL

Much like his previous school, Charles found that Carlisle was also set up like a military institute. When he and his brother arrived, they were made to pose for a "before" photograph. They were then given a bath, a haircut, and a uniform and had to stand for another photograph as an "after." This was done for all new students to show how they were being changed from "savage" to "civilized." Some students who didn't have English names were made to choose a new name from a blackboard. Luckily, Charles and his brother already had English names because their father was white.

Students who came to Carlisle were forbidden to speak their Native languages. They could only use English. The teachers also watched them to make sure they did not socialize with other students from their home nation, even if they were their brothers and sisters.

The Carlisle school was primarily a vocational training school. Students spent half of each day studying reading, writing, and math. They spent the other half of the day learning a trade. Learning a trade was seen as a way to "civilize" the students and make them future productive citizens. They had to work hard. Some boys learned to become farmers. They learned how to choose and plant crops, drive tractors, fix equipment, and milk cows. Their day started very early. Other students were taught how to make shoes. They worked long hours making boots and shoes that were sold to the nearby military

base. Some of the other skills taught at Carlisle included carpentry, plumbing, tailoring, and printing.

Unlike the boys, the female students were not taught job skills. Instead, they were taught to be good wives and mothers. They learned skills such as sewing, dressmaking, laundry, cooking, and childcare. Some of the more promising girls were taught to be nurses. The students were told they needed these skills so they could become like the white man and support their families. They were reminded that their land was gone and they could no longer hunt and fish for a living.

As students approached graduation, they were sent to live with a white family for one year. During that year, students would attend school and work in their given trade. This practice was called an "outing." It was hoped some of the students would model the behaviors of their host families.

Chapter Four

SPORTS

While the Carlisle school was very strict, it did offer some fun for the students. Although academics were the school's primary focus, students had many extracurricular activities to choose from. Students could participate in music, speech, journalism, arts and crafts, and join various sports teams. It was sports that made Carlisle famous, and what helped turn Charles Bender into a legend.

Athletics were very popular at Carlisle. The school's leaders thought sports were a great way to help "civilize" the student athletes. Sports also kept the students busy. For the students, sports were a welcomed social activity. They could play games with their friends and enjoy time away from classroom work and learning their trades.

Sports such as football, basketball, and baseball were very popular. Football was the most popular, because it was coached by the legendary Glenn "Pop" Warner. During his time at Carlisle, Warner coached many students who excelled at their given sports. This included famous professional football player and Olympic gold medalist Jim Thorpe of the Sac and Fox Nation. He became legendary for his skill on the football field and in track and field events.

Even though he would eventually become a legendary athlete himself, Charles was not immediately interested in sports. For his first two years at school, he focused on his classwork and learned his trade as a watchmaker. It wasn't until 1898 that he finally decided to join sports.

One day, when he was sixteen, Charles was hanging around the gym with his friends. They needed someone to throw them pitches for practice, so Charles decided to give a few throws. Having developed a good arm from throwing rocks in the fields back in White Earth, he was a natural. His pitches zoomed! His natural skill caught the eye of Coach Pop Warner, who noticed Charles's talent immediately. Warner quickly asked him to join the varsity baseball team.

Starting in 1898, Charles starred on the team as a pitcher and second baseman. He helped his team become very successful in games against white high schools and colleges across Pennsylvania. Charles was a successful player and a good student. He kept up with his studies and was a model for others through his hard work and dedication.

As his graduation day approached in 1901, Charles was faced with a decision. He was trained to go directly to work in his trade, but he thought he might want to go to college instead. Nearby was a place called Dickinson College, which offered a special opportunity. The college had a program that accepted select Native American students to attend pre-college. Charles loved school and attended classes for one year. Even though he enjoyed it, there wasn't an opportunity for him to play baseball there. He finally left school in 1902 and joined a semi-professional team in nearby Harrisburg.

Chapter Five

AN UP-AND-COMING PROSPECT

During the summer of 1902 at Harrisburg, Charles got his first taste of competitive baseball. He pitched and played in the field, and he enjoyed the challenge of playing against good players from around the country. The highlight of his time with Harrisburg was an exhibition game against the Major League Chicago Cubs, who were playing games against semi-pros to hone their skills in the off-season. Charles was chosen to pitch against the Cubs. He did his best and held his own against the professional stars, but he lost the game. Charles was sad, but his skill was noticed by a scout from the Philadelphia Athletics who had attended to watch the Cubs in action. He immediately reported to the Athletics' manager, Connie Mack, that there was an amazing talent pitching for Harrisburg.

Mack was interested and soon went to watch Charles in action for himself. He was impressed! Mack decided on the spot to offer Charles a contract to come pitch for the Athletics as a professional. He signed for a princely sum of $1,800 (about $50,000 in today's money).

Only nineteen years old, Charles was a new player, a rookie with the Athletics. While it was only natural for a kid fresh out of high school to be scared by the pressure of professional sports, Charles was a warrior. In his very first game, he pitched amazingly well. He was called in to finish the game when the starting pitcher floundered. He pitched six innings and won the game over the legendary Cy Young

of the Boston Americans (later the Red Sox). Impressed with his calm and collected skill, Coach Mack decided to let Charles start the next game. He went toe to toe with future Hall of Fame pitcher Clark Griffith of the New York Highlanders. He won the game with a complete game shutout!

While he had ups and downs throughout the 1903 season, Charles started in thirty-three games. He completed twenty-nine of them. He won seventeen games against fourteen losses and only allowed a bit over three runs a game. His team finished second in the league and Charles was considered to have had one of the finest rookie seasons in baseball.

Chapter Six

A NEW ACE

Heading into the 1904 season, expectations were high for the Athletics. They were even higher for the flashy, young pitching sensation that Charles was during the 1903 season. Unfortunately, Charles struggled with what some people call a sophomore slump. He was impressive in a few of his starts, but overall he had a less than good year. Even though he only allowed about one hit per inning and less than three runs a game, his team batted poorly and finished in fifth place. Charles only won ten games and lost eleven. Despite this, Coach Mack thought Charles had gained good experience. He encouraged him to practice harder and Charles took the advice. He looked forward to the next season.

1905 was a breakout year for Charles. He listened to what Coach Mack told him and put his poor season behind him. He put more power into his pitches and was healthier than 1904. He pitched about seven innings each game he started. He won a whopping eighteen games that year and was very reliable when asked to fill in as a reliever. As a starter, Charles completed eighteen games out of twenty-three starts. He finished twelve games for other pitchers. His skills were valuable, and over the season the Athletics were a powerhouse. They scored almost a hundred more runs than the year before. When the season ended, they were in first place.

Finishing in first place meant the Athletics would be in the World Series in 1905. Their opponent was the powerhouse New York

Giants team, who had won a whopping 105 games. The Giants were favored to win the series easily, and most people thought they would make fast work of the Athletics. During the first game, the Giants soundly beat the Athletics with a shutout by the legendary Christy Mathewson. Charles was named to start game two of the series.

Everyone figured the young Native American pitcher would lose. He was facing the legendary Joe McGinnty, who had won twenty-five games that year. Coach Mack gave his team a pep talk and took young Charles to the side. He said he believed in him and that all he needed to do was relax and do his best. Charles didn't want to disappoint his team or his coach. Over the first two innings, Charles held steady—neck and neck with McGinnty. Then, in the third inning, the Athletics scored a run. That was all Charles needed. He shut the Giants out over the rest of the game. He allowed only four hits and struck out nine batters. He didn't allow a single run!

Unfortunately, that win by Charles was the only win the Athletics would get in the World Series that year. Charles pitched again in game seven, but he lost a close game to Mathewson. The Athletics lost the series, five games to one.

It was during the 1905 World Series that the press began to call him Chief, because he was Native American. In an interview with *The Sporting News* after the World Series, he was asked about his Ojibwe heritage. Even though he was proud of who he was and where he came from, Charles told the reporter, "I do not want my name to be presented to the public as an Indian, but as a pitcher." Even so, the nickname Chief stuck with him his whole life.

Chapter Seven

THE LEARNING CURVE: INVENTING THE SLIDER

Not to be troubled by the loss during the 1905 World Series, Charles decided he would learn from it. Having faced the legendary Christy Mathewson twice, he wanted to improve his game. He worked hard over the off-season, developing more control over his pitches and learning how to throw different pitches that would be better against opposing batters.

As a good student and a fast learner, Charles learned to throw a fadeaway screwball that looked like a straight pitch, but actually moved toward the batter to fool them. After mastering this pitch, he started to experiment with improving different techniques and variations. Knowing that some people could key in on slow curveball pitches, Charles created a new pitch! It was a sharp, fast-breaking curveball that he called a "slider." The slider pitch was a curveball with a new twist. By throwing hard to look like a regular fastball, and by gripping the ball differently, Charles could make it "slide" at the end to move away from the batter. Nobody had ever thought to throw the ball like this before.

Later in life, when asked how he created the slider, Charles mentioned how he used to experiment as a pitcher. He said, "I used fast curves, pitched overhand and sidearm, fastballs, high and inside, and an underhand fadeaway pitch with the hand almost down to the level

of the knees." His ability to throw so many different pitches made it so difficult for batters to hit against him.

Armed with his new pitches and his experience in the World Series, Charles entered the 1906 season with high hopes. He did his best and lowered the number of runs he allowed in games to about two and a half per game. Unfortunately, the rest of the team slipped and the Athletics finished a dismal fourth place, but Charles had earned a place as one of the aces of the Athletics for years to come.

Chapter Eight

RACISM AND REDEMPTION

T he year 1907 was an improvement over 1906. The Athletics got better and finished second place in their division. They put on an impressive run, but finished just behind the Detroit Tigers. Charles won sixteen games that year and lowered his runs allowed per game to almost two, and he allowed less than one hit per inning. A fantastic feat, indeed.

Even though his fame was spreading on the baseball diamond, he still faced racism as a Native American. During a series in Washington, DC, Charles had the afternoon off. He decided to look around the city. He spent the day window-shopping, looking at the city's great monuments and at the White House, and after a while he became thirsty. Deciding to get a cool drink, Charles went into a malt and soda shop. He asked the owner for a lemon seltzer. Instead of serving him his drink, the man yelled at Charles, "Get out! You're not allowed." Charles was surprised. He was taught at the Carlisle School that an educated Native American was as good as a white man. He repeated his order. The man ignored his request and called for help from another worker. Together, they grabbed poor Charles and threw him out and onto the ground. While he was used to people making war whoops at games, people calling him Chief in the press, and racist cartoons made about him, this was the first time he faced violent racism.

Finishing in second place raised hopes in Philadelphia for the up-

coming season. Instead, 1908 turned out to be a disappointment. The Athletics lost eighty-five games and only won sixty-eight. Charles was injured much of the year and only pitched in eighteen games. He won nine of his games and lowered his earned runs to under two per game, but he didn't make a very impressive impact on the field.

The next year, 1909, was a bounce-back year for Charles and the Athletics. They improved so much that they nearly took first place in their division. Charles also improved. He won eighteen games and allowed the seventh lowest number of runs scored. He was healthy and pitched 250 innings over thirty-four games. His reliability was rewarded as he was moved up to be the number-two pitcher in the Athletics rotation that year.

Chapter Nine

AWW, SHOOT!

During his off-seasons and between games, Charles was addicted to being outdoors. He was known to take long walks in the different cities where his team played. Seeing the sights in the great cities out east was a treat for a kid from Minnesota.

He also started golfing for enjoyment. It was a sport that required skill and precision. It also allowed Charles to get far away from crowds and the racism that followed him when he was on the road. This didn't go unnoticed. One of his teammates, Eddie Collins, remembered how Charles enjoyed golf: "You will never find Chief Bender, our Indian pitcher, hanging around the hotel. Too many fans are apt to salute him with a war whoop. Besides, he is golf mad and when not on the diamond, he is to be found on the links . . ."

Charles was also an avid trap shotgun shooter. Trapshooting was a popular sport that developed in the late nineteenth century. It requires a twelve-gauge shotgun used to shoot clay saucer-shaped targets that are launched into the sky in front of the shooter. The object is to shoot as many targets as possible before they fall to the ground. It was originally a way for hunters to practice shooting at birds when it wasn't hunting season. This is why the clay targets are often called clay pigeons. A lot of famous baseball players were introduced to the sport as a way to create interest. Some of the people who were recruited were famous players who eventually became Hall of Fame members. Some of the participants included pitchers Christy

Mathewson and Grover Cleveland Alexander; hitters such as Ty Cobb, Honus Wagner, Eddie Collins, and Frank "Home Run" Baker; and (of course) Charles Bender.

Having grown up on the White Earth Reservation, where hunting was a way of life, Charles had a knack for trapshooting. Soon, he was winning competitions and was almost as famous as a shooter as he was as a ballplayer. He made good money from his winnings as a shooter too. In 1909, he was paid $1,800 for pitching for the Athletics, but he made $1,200 from trapshooting (about $35,000 today).

Charles also made money as a spokesman for the sport of trap-shooting. His fame as a ballplayer and a shooter made him a great candidate for advertisements for shooting competitions and rifles. Companies paid him very well, and that year he made more money from shooting and appearing in advertisements than he did playing baseball.

Chapter Ten

THE WORLD SERIES

The 1910 season was a magical season for Charles and the Athletics. They had improved in 1909 and expectations were high that they would do well. But they did more than well—they did great!

That year, the Athletics were an absolute powerhouse in their division. Charles himself was astounding. He started the season hot and stayed that way for most of the year. He won fourteen straight games and even threw a no-hitter on May 12. His twenty-five wins that year were the fourth best in the league, and his earned run average was fifth best. The Athletics swept their way to 102 wins and were fourteen and a half games better than the second-place team.

In the World Series that year, Charles was tapped by manager Connie Mack to start the first game against the Cubs. This was an extreme honor. Charles was nervous, but he was confident in his skills. The game started with a bang. The Athletics scored two runs in the second inning and another in the third. Frank Baker had three hits and two RBIs (runs batted in). That was all Charles needed. He went on to pitch a gem of a game. He held the Cubs to only three hits the entire game. Victory was assured and Charles allowed only one unearned run in the ninth inning.

The Athletics won the next two games handily, nine runs to three, and twelve runs to five. In the fourth game, Charles had the chance to close out the series if he won. He pitched a great game. The Athletics were ahead 3–2 in the bottom of the ninth inning. Charles was only

three outs away from winning the World Series for his team, but a momentary lapse allowed the Cubs to tie the game. He then allowed a run in the tenth inning and lost the game. Fortunately, the Athletics won the next game—and they won the World Series too.

Losing that one game to the Cubs was a devastating blow to Charles, but his teammates rallied around him. His manager congratulated him for his fine pitching performance.

"How much do you owe on your house?" Mack asked Charles.

"None of your business," Charles said.

Mack pressed the issue and asked again. Charles finally gave in and told him how much he still owed. To Charles's surprise, Mack offered him a raise in salary equal to what he owed on the house, so he could pay it off.

Chapter Eleven

THE KING OF THE DYNASTY

Expectations were high heading into the 1911 season. Coach Connie Mack kept his core players happy in the off-season with increased salaries, and things started out with a shot once spring training rolled around. The team was excited for the new season and everyone was ready to win it all again—especially Charles.

The Athletics started off hot and never looked back. They led the league all season long. Charles himself was confident in his stuff, and it showed. He pitched in thirty-four games for the Athletics that year. He started in twenty-five of them, and he won seventeen games and lost only five! It was, by far, his best season. Everyone was impressed by his skill and poise. He was becoming known more for his skills and less because people were curious about a Native American pitcher in the Major League.

In the first game of the 1911 World Series, Charles lost a close game to eventual Hall of Famer Christy Mathewson. Charles allowed only two runs (one earned), but Mathewson threw a gem and allowed only one run to the Athletics. The Athletics won the next two games and took the lead in the series. In game four, Charles allowed only two runs and won the game for the Athletics. Things looked up for them, but they lost the next game in a close battle.

Hoping to close out the series in game six, Coach Mack looked at his choices. He knew Charles had pitched only two days before and might still be tired. But he was sure Charles could get the job done. He was right. Charles pitched the Athletics to the win in the World Series. He pitched a complete game and sealed it. His pitching at the World Series was hailed as one of the most impressive feats in baseball by striking out twenty batters in twenty-six innings and only allowing one earned run average in the three games he pitched.

The next year was a bit of a letdown after the impressive season of 1911. The Athletics struggled to third place in their division, and Charles was injured for part of the season. When he did pitch, he had a few problems. While he won thirteen games that year, he lost eight, and his earned run average was nearly three runs per game. He pitched only 171 innings over the entire season in 1912.

Over the course of the off-season, Charles worked hard to be in top shape for the 1913 season. He came into spring looking forward to redeeming himself and helping his team improve. He didn't disappoint. That summer, Charles was a true powerhouse. He pitched in forty-eight games—the most on the team. He started twenty-one games and completed fourteen of them. As a relief pitcher, Charles appeared in twenty-four games and saved thirteen of them. Overall, he accounted for thirty-four of his team's ninety-five wins: twenty-one as a starter and thirteen as a reliever. Charles also lowered the number of runs allowed in his games to almost two. The Athletics easily cruised to first place and were matched against the New York Giants in the 1913 World Series. Coach Mack knew who he could rely on. He started Charles in games one and four. Charles did not disappoint. He won both games by close margins and completed both. The team easily cruised to the series victory in five games.

Later, recalling just how important Charles was to the Athletics in 1911 and 1913, Coach Mack made an interesting observation. Coach

Mack had always called Charles by his middle name, Albert. "If I had all the men I've ever handled and they were in their prime and there was one game I wanted to win above all others, Albert would be my man," he said.

Many reporters and sports fans were calling the Athletics a dynasty. They had won three World Series in the past four years. Coming into 1914, the Athletics were favorites to win it all again. Although he was injured for parts of the year, Charles performed in near-perfect fashion. He won seventeen games and lost only three. His earned run average was near two runs a game and he struck out twice as many players as he walked that year. The Athletics again took first place and were favored to win against the Boston Braves in the World Series, but fate worked against the Athletics when they were swept in four games. Charles himself was soundly beaten in game one of the series. It was the worst performance of his career.

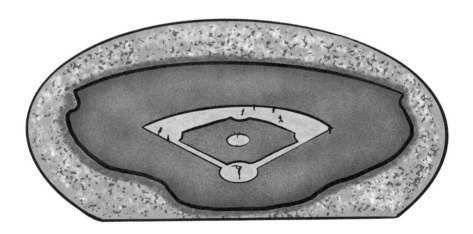

Chapter Twelve

JUMPING THE FENCE

Following the 1914 season, in 1915, Charles was a bit upset when his request for a higher salary was ignored by Coach Mack. He felt he had proven his worth to the team during his career and wanted to get a pay raise to match the hard work and winning track record he had established for the Athletics. Unfortunately, Mack wouldn't budge.

That year, the upstart Federal League, a competing baseball league, started to offer Major League stars huge sums of money to come play for their teams. Charles was a hot commodity and he was offered $8,000 (about $200,000 today) to play for the Baltimore Terrapins. This was much more than he had ever made playing for the Athletics, so he took the offer. It was an offer he immediately regretted. While the grass looked greener on the other side, he found out it wasn't the same.

Having played for a supportive coach his entire career, Charles found that his new team was not player friendly. The talent in the new league was different and he didn't have the familiar crowds and stadium he had grown used to. He was also thirty-one years old and a lifetime of hard throwing was beginning to take a toll on his arm. He won only four games for the Terrapins and lost sixteen. His earned run average was almost four runs per game. Disillusioned, Charles sought to return to the Athletics, but budget constraints kept him from coming back.

In 1916, Charles accepted a contract from the Philadelphia Phillies. Although he was still not an Athletic, Charles was happy to have returned to his adopted hometown. He improved slightly over his dismal 1915 season. He won seven games and lost seven games. His earned run average remained near four runs per game and he pitched only 122 innings that season.

The Phillies finished dead last. The next year, 1917, was equally dismal for Charles. Although both he and the team improved, his health limited him to only 113 innings that year. Even though he won eight games, lost two, and lowered his earned run average to less than two runs per game, he considered the season a failure. He was released by the Phillies and he retired at the end of 1917. He hoped to get back on the Athletics, but Coach Mack didn't extend an offer to him.

Chapter Thirteen

LIFE AFTER THE PROS

With his baseball career over, Charles took work in 1918 at the Philadelphia shipyards. World War I was in its final days and he decided it was his duty to contribute to the war effort and to earn a living to support his wife, Marie, and their household.

Once the war ended, Charles looked to get back into baseball. He was hired to manage the Richmond Colts, a minor league team in Richmond, Virginia. In addition to his coaching duties, Charles also put his skills to work as an occasional pitcher for the Colts. As a former Major League star, Charles dominated at the minor league level. In 1919, he won twenty-nine games, lost two, and had an earned run average just above one run per game. His team won the league. His impressive showing piqued the interest of some Major League teams, but he was making as much money as a manager in the minors as he would as a player in the majors, so Charles decided against a return to the Majors as a player.

During the 1920–21 seasons, he was a player/coach for the New Haven Indians. They were excited to have the great Chief Bender as their coach. He won twenty-five games in 1920 and fourteen games in 1921 as a pitcher. His team took first place in 1920 and fourth in 1921.

After New Haven, Charles played and coached for the Reading Aces (1922), the Baltimore Orioles (1923), the New Haven Profs (1923), and the Johnstown Johnnies (1924).

In 1925, when he was forty-three years old, his old pal Eddie Collins hired Charles to be an assistant coach for the Chicago White Sox. He was able to share his experience with some of the young players, and he got one last taste of big-league ball. Collins talked Charles into pitching one last Major League game. He dug deep into his bag of tricks, but age had caught up to him at last. Charles allowed two runs in one inning of work. After that, he hung up his cleats and retired from playing for good.

Chapter Fourteen

RETIREMENT

During the 1930s, Charles opened a sporting goods store in Philadelphia as a way to make ends meet. He occasionally took side jobs as a coach and baseball consultant during the summers to earn extra money. He managed the Erie Sailors in 1932, and was a coach for the US Naval Academy that same year.

Even as he got older, Charles's baseball knowledge was still sought after by many Major League teams. He was hired by teams such as the Chicago White Sox, New York Yankees, and New York Giants as a pitching coach and as a scout to help them find new pitchers. When he was sixty-one years old, his old Athletics team hired him to pitch batting practice to their players and to mentor their young and upcoming pitchers. Charles was always ready to share his wisdom and to help young players grow.

In his retirement, Charles also learned to enjoy things outside of baseball. He still enjoyed shooting, and he loved to hunt and fish. When he could, he would return to his land at the White Earth Reservation to shoot partridges, a small game bird common in northwestern Minnesota. He also became a very good golfer and learned to play pool like a shark. But, by far, Charles's favorite hobbies were gardening and painting oil landscapes of the beautiful world around him. All of these ventures allowed him to get outside and enjoy the

beauty of the natural world he had loved since his childhood growing up in Minnesota.

When Charles was seventy-one years old, in 1953, he was finally elected to the National Baseball Hall of Fame. He lived long enough to enjoy recognition as one of baseball's greatest pitchers, and he was the first Minnesotan to be elected to the Hall of Fame.

Over his career, Charles won 212 regular season games and six World Series games. He won over 62 percent of the games he pitched in, and his career earned run average was an amazing 2.46!

CHARLES BENDER CAREER STATISTICS

Year	Age	Tm	W	L	SV	ERA	BB	SO
1903	19	PHA	17	14	0	3.07	65	127
1904	20	PHA	10	11	0	2.87	59	149
1905	21	PHA	18	11	0	2.83	90	142
1906	22	PHA	15	10	3	2.53	48	159
1907	23	PHA	16	8	3	2.05	34	112
1908	24	PHA	8	9	1	1.75	21	85
1909	25	PHA	18	8	1	1.66	45	161
1910	26	PHA	23	5	0	1.58	47	155
1911	27	PHA	17	5	3	2.16	58	114
1912	28	PHA	13	8	2	2.74	33	90
1913	29	PHA	21	10	13	2.21	59	135
1914	30	PHA	17	3	2	2.26	55	107
1915	31	BAL	4	16	1	3.99	37	89
1916	32	PHI	7	7	3	3.74	34	43
1917	33	PHI	8	2	2	1.67	26	43
1925	41	CHW	0	0	0	18	1	0
16 Yrs			212	127	34	2.46	712	1711

The life of Charles Bender was an amazing example of how you can overcome the proverbial curveballs that life throws at you by working hard, honing your skills, and giving it everything you have. Even though he started life on the shores of a small lake, grew up in poverty on the reservation, and suffered from racism, he never let that get him down or define him. He is a clear example of how to live your life. This is summed up in a quote he once said:

"You give the best you have—you win or lose.
What's the difference if you give all you've got to give?"

EXTEND YOUR LEARNING

The activities and additional information in the following pages are intended for use with the Charles Albert Bender, Ella Cara Deloria, and Peggy Flanagan books in the Minnesota Native Lives Series.

IDEAS FOR WRITING AND DISCUSSION

What Do You Think?

- What moment in this story do you think you will most remember? Why?

- Who do you believe was most important to this person's success? Why?

- What do you think were the hardest moments for this person? Why?

- How do you think this person was able to overcome hardship in their life?

- What were the happiest moments in the story of this person's life?

- What are some of the happiest moments in your life?

- What moment in the story reminded you of something in your own life?

- Write your own short autobiography, the story of your life so far, told by you!

IDEAS FOR VISUAL PROJECTS

Show Us What You Think

- Draw images for three or four moments that are not illustrated in this book.

- Draw a sketch of this person and include items they liked.

- Find images from American Indian boarding schools from the time this book covers.

- Find historic images to share of activities the book mentions. Are they different now?

- Find historic images to share of the reservations or places the book mentions.

- Make a map of the eleven tribal nations within the boundaries of the state of Minnesota. Where are they located? What tribe lives there? What else did you learn?

- Give a visual presentation on how treaties formed the White Earth Reservation, homeland of both Charles Albert Bender amd Peggy Flanagan. Explore "Why Treaties Matter" for information.

- Create a bar graph or pie chart or other infographic on one of these topics:

  1. How many Native Americans live in urban areas of Minnesota? Which cities in Minnesota are home to the largest populations of Native Americans?

  2. Many Native American students attend school in Minnesota—you may be one of them. How many Native American students are in your school district? How many tribes are represented?

Resources

- Minnesota Indian Education—Teaching and Learning: www.education.mn.gov/MDE/dse/indian/teach

- Why Treaties Matter: www.treatiesmatter.org/exhibit/wp-content/uploads/2017/09/Updated-Sovereign-Nations1.pdf

IDEAS FOR FURTHER LEARNING

Dakota and Ojibwe people continue to live in Minnesota and are part of all aspects of our society. While English is a shared language, many Dakota and Ojibwe people also study and speak their Indigenous languages called Dakota and Anishinaabemowin.

Find Out More

- Find unfamiliar words in this book and create a glossary or word list with their definitions.

- Create a timeline for this person's life. Add dates from the timeline on page 51.

- Learn how to count to ten in Dakota or Ojibwe.

- Look up Ojibwe or Dakota words for baseball or ball games such as lacrosse.

- Learn about Dakota and Ojibwe sports and activities, such as powwows.

- Make a list of four common traditions the Ojibwe and Dakota share.

Resources

- Ojibwe People's Dictionary: ojibwe.lib.umn.edu

- Beginning Dakota: www.beginningdakota.org

- In Honor of the People: www.inhonorofthepeople.org

- Minnesota Historical Society, Minnesota Territory: www.mnhs.org/talesoftheterritory

- Ojibwe Material Culture: www.mnhs.org/ojibwematerialculture

- Oceti Sakowiŋ, The Seven Council Fires: www.mnhs.org/sevencouncilfires

Historical Context

Dakota and Ojibwe people live in today's context of the twenty-first century. We also have histories as rich and full of struggle as the US or other countries. This timeline presents important events in one place as a reminder that no one human history is more important than another, but history often makes it look that way. This timeline also provides context from Dakota and Ojibwe history. You can use it to respond to the books in this series by comparing each person's timeline and history to the events listed here.

Beyond memory, this place called Mni Sota Makoce, or Minnesota, is where the people became Dakota. They traveled as far north as Hudson Bay, as far west as the Rocky Mountains, south to trade with the Pueblos, and past the trading city of Cahokia, to the southeastern part of what later became the United States.

During this same time, Anishinaabeg, the larger group that includes Ojibwe people, lived far to the east of Minnesota, near the Atlantic Ocean. A series of prophecies, or visions of their future, set the Ojibwe off on their five-hundred-year journey to find a new home in "a land where food grows on water" (meaning manoomin, wild rice) along the Great Lakes and eventually in Minnesota.

TIMELINE

900 Dakota live, as they have always, in what will become Minnesota; ancestors of the Ojibwe begin migrating west to find a new homeland that was foretold in a vision.

1400 Ancestors of the Ojibwe reach the northwestern area of what later becomes Minnesota.

1540s Spanish explorers map the Mississippi River and Dakota village sites.

1622 Ojibwe make contact with French explorer Étienne Brûlé at Lake Superior.

1689 Ojibwe fight for the French against the British until 1763 in what is now the US and Canada.

1730s Ojibwe and Dakota begin battles over Dakota territories that end in the 1850s.

1769 Dartmouth College is founded to educate Native Americans in Christian theology.

1783 The American Revolution ends.

1805 Zebulon Pike and Dakota sign an agreement to sell land to the Americans in present-day Minneapolis. The Dakota are never paid for the land.

1812	Ojibwe and Dakota fight on the side of the British in the War of 1812.
1816	Saswe, Ella Cara Deloria's grandfather, is born in what is now Minnesota.
1819	Americans build a fort at Bdote (where the rivers meet in present-day St. Paul).
1825	Dakota and Ojibwe leaders and other tribes sign the Prairie du Chien Treaty and lose their land.
1830	Congress passes the Indian Removal Act. All Native Americans are required to move west of the Mississippi River. Many tribes remain in their homelands. Some are marched by force hundreds of miles from their homelands.
1837	A series of treaties begins where both Dakota and Ojibwe peoples' lands are taken away and many are forced to move.
1849	Minnesota Territory begins a period of organization (claiming) by the US that lasts until 1858.
1850s	Treaties require Dakota and Ojibwe to let go of hundreds of millions of acres of land.
1853	The 1851 treaties are ratified; American settlers encroach on Dakota lands.
1858	Minnesota becomes a state.
1858	Pay shah de o quay/Mary Razor, mother of Charles Albert Bender, is born.
1861	The American Civil War begins.

1862	War between the Dakota and the US begins in August. The fighting lasts six weeks.
1862	The Dakota ask the Ojibwe to protect their big drum during the war with the US.
1863	Treaties with Dakota people are repealed and almost all Dakota are removed from Minnesota.
1865	The American Civil War ends.
1867	The White Earth Reservation is established.
1870	Dakota and Ojibwe sign a peace treaty that remains unbroken.
1879	Colonel Richard Pratt founds the Carlisle Indian Boarding School.
1880s	Dakota people return to their communities in Minnesota.
1884	Charles Albert Bender is born in Brainerd, Minnesota.
1884	The Haskell Institute opens as a boarding school for Native American children.
1889	Ella Cara Deloria is born on the Yankton Reservation in South Dakota.
1902	Charles Albert Bender graduates from the Carlisle Indian School in Pennsylvania.
1914	Ella Cara Deloria graduates from Columbia University with a bachelor's degree in education.
1924	The Indian Citizenship Act of Congress grants citizenship to all Native Americans.

1925	Charles Albert Bender retires from professional baseball.
1932	Ella Cara Deloria publishes *Dakota Texts*.
1934	The Indian Reorganization Act is passed, forcing tribes to all operate by the same government model.
1944	Ella Cara Deloria publishes *Speaking of Indians*.
1953	Charles Albert Bender is inducted into the National Baseball Hall of Fame.
1953	The Termination Resolution by Congress is passed, intending to end US recognition of tribes.
1954	Charles Albert Bender dies in Pennsylvania.
1956	The Indian Relocation Act is passed to move Native Americans off reservations and into cities.
1971	Ella Cara Deloria dies in South Dakota.
1978	The Religious Freedom Act is passed, ending laws against religious and cultural practices of tribes.
1979	Peggy Flanagan is born in St. Louis Park, Minnesota.
1988	Ella Cara Deloria's *Waterlily* is published.
2007	Ella Cara Deloria's *The Dakota Way of Life* is published.
2019	Peggy Flanagan is sworn in as lieutenant governor of Minnesota, making her the highest-ranking Native American woman elected to an executive office in the United States.

ABOUT THE AUTHOR

Kade Ferris is an anthropologist and historian with over twenty-five years of experience working with Ojibwe and other tribal communities across the upper Midwest.

Kade received a bachelor's degree in anthropology from the University of North Dakota and a master's degree in anthropology from North Dakota State University. His research focuses on the history and culture of the Anishinaabe people. Kade has written several books and maintains a historical website, dibaajimowin.com, which chronicles small, interesting stories that can be used to learn more about the unique history and culture of the Indigenous peoples of Minnesota, North Dakota, and southern Canada.

Kade is of Turtle Mountain Chippewa and Canadian Metis descent. He is a proud husband and father of five sons. He presently resides in Minnesota, where he continues his work with the Ojibwe people in tribal cultural preservation efforts.

ABOUT THE ILLUSTRATOR

Tashia Hart grew up in the wilds of Minnesota. She loves animals, writing, drawing, plants, and cooking. She is the author of *Gidjie and the Wolves* (Intermediaries, volume 1) and *Girl Unreserved* (Broken Wings and Things, volume 1). Her forthcoming wild rice cookbook, in partnership with the Minnesota Historical Society Press, is set to be released in the fall of 2021. She writes essays and recipes about wild foods for various organizations and tribal programs, and is an avid beader with thirty years of experience. She believes Indigenous people should control how their stories and likenesses are portrayed, and so has recently started the independent publishing company (Not) Too Far Removed Press. The mission of the press is to uplift fellow Indigenous authors and artists of the Midwest region. Tashia is Red Lake Anishinaabe. www.tashiahart.com

ABOUT THE SERIES EDITORS

Heid E. Erdrich is Ojibwe enrolled at the Turtle Mountain Reservation in North Dakota. She grew up in Wahpeton, North Dakota, not far from the White Earth Reservation in Minnesota and the Sisseton-Wahpeton Reservation in South Dakota. Her neighbors in her hometown were Dakota and Ojibwe from these tribal nations. Heid is the author of seven collections of poetry and a cookbook focused on indigenous foods of Minnesota and neighboring states titled *Original Local*. Her writing has won fellowships and awards from the National Poetry Series, Native Arts and Cultures Foundation, Minnesota State Arts Board, and more. She has twice won a Minnesota Book Award for poetry. A longtime teacher of writing at colleges and universities, Heid enjoys editing. She edited the anthologies *New Poets of Native Nations* from Graywolf Press, and *Sister Nations* from the Minnesota Historical Society Press. Heid's new poetry collection is *Little Big Bully*, Penguin Editions, 2020. Along with being Anishinaabe/Ojibwe, Heid's extended family includes Anishinaabe from several bands, Dakota, Hidatsa, Somali American, German American, and immigrants from India and elsewhere. She is also Metis, a group of people whose ancestors were French and Native American, and who lived in what became the United States and Canada. She loves the Great Lakes area and calls it home. Heid has lived in Minnesota for many years, raising her kids in Minneapolis, where they went to public schools. She enjoyed working with the authors and editors of this series of biographies and hopes you will read and reread these books!

Gwen Nell Westerman is Dakota and enrolled with the Sisseton Wahpeton Oyate in South Dakota. She is also a citizen of the Cherokee Nation. Her parents went to boarding schools in Oklahoma and South Dakota, and met at the Haskell Institute in Lawrence, Kansas. Gwen grew up in Oklahoma and Kansas among many different tribal nations. One of her earliest memories is when she was three, scribbling in a book. Her mother asked what she was doing and Gwen said, "I'm writing!" Today, she writes about Dakota history and language. She has won two Minnesota Book Awards for her work about Dakota people. Gwen's first poetry book was written in English and Dakota. Her poems have been published in anthologies, and so have her art quilts. Her quilt art received awards from the Minnesota State Arts Board, the Minnesota Historical Society, the Great Plains Art Museum, and the Heard Museum, and has been exhibited in many places across the United States. Her children were born in Oklahoma and grew up in Minnesota. Gwen's family tree includes teachers, leaders, and hard workers who were Dakota, Ojibwe, Odawa, and Cherokee, along with a few French and Scottish traders. She knows the names of all her ancestors on both sides of her family back before the American Revolution. She lives in Minnesota with her husband and their little black dog. She hopes you enjoy reading these books as much as she liked working on them, and that you will share them with your friends and families.